Neighborhood Safari

Skunks

by Dalton Rains

FOCUS READERS®
PIONEER

www.focusreaders.com

Focus Readers is distributed by North Star Editions:
sales@northstareditions.com | 888-417-0195

Produced for Focus Readers by Red Line Editorial.

Photographs ©: Shutterstock Images, cover, 1, 4, 6, 8, 10, 12, 14, 17, 18, 21

Library of Congress Cataloging-in-Publication Data
Names: Rains, Dalton, author.
Title: Skunks / by Dalton Rains.
Description: Mendota Heights, MN: Focus Readers, [2025] | Series: Neighborhood safari | Includes bibliographical references and index. | Audience: Grades K-1
Identifiers: LCCN 2024002181 (print) | LCCN 2024002182 (ebook) | ISBN 9798889981794 (hardcover) | ISBN 9798889982357 (paperback) | ISBN 9798889983460 (pdf) | ISBN 9798889982913 (ebook)
Subjects: LCSH: Skunks--Juvenile literature.
Classification: LCC QL737.C248 R35 2025 (print) | LCC QL737.C248 (ebook) | DDC 599.76/8--dc23/eng/20240311
LC record available at https://lccn.loc.gov/2024002181
LC ebook record available at https://lccn.loc.gov/2024002182

Printed in the United States of America
Mankato, MN
082024

About the Author

Dalton Rains is a writer and editor from Minnesota.

Table of Contents

Chapter 1

Smelly Skunks

A coyote runs toward a skunk. The skunk raises its tail. But the coyote comes closer. The skunk sprays the **predator** with a smelly **liquid**. The coyote runs away. The skunk is safe.

Skunks can live in many kinds of places. They are often found in open areas. Most skunks make their homes in **dens**. Some skunks move into dens left behind by other animals. Other skunks dig their own.

Skunks live alone for most of the year. They only come together to **mate**.

Chapter 2

Body Parts

Skunks are **mammals**. They have black fur on most of their bodies. Some kinds of skunks have white stripes on their backs. Others have white spots or swirls.

tail
claw
nose
leg
fur

Skunks have long noses. They have strong legs. They have long claws, too. Skunks also have **glands** under their tails. These glands make a stinky spray.

Most skunks are the size of a house cat. But the smallest skunks can fit in a person's hand.

Chapter 3

Staying Safe

A skunk's strong legs help it dig. The legs also help the skunk move over rough ground. Some skunks can even climb trees.

A skunk's black-and-white fur acts as a warning. The fur tells predators to stay away. If an animal comes close, the skunk may spray it. The skunk may aim at the animal's eyes. Or the skunk may send out a large cloud.

Some skunks stand on their front legs as they spray.

Using Spray

Skunks use spray to keep predators away. The spray can **blind** animals. But skunks try not to use it often. The spray can take more than a week to refill. So, skunks try to scare animals instead. They stomp their feet and raise their tails.

Chapter 4

A Skunk's Life

Skunks mate in the spring. Babies are born two months later. Most **litters** have four to six babies. At first, the babies cannot see.

Three weeks after birth, baby skunks open their eyes. They go outside the den after six weeks. Mothers teach the young skunks to hunt. Males leave their mother after a few months. Females may stay for up to a year.

Wild skunks can live six years or more.

Life Cycle

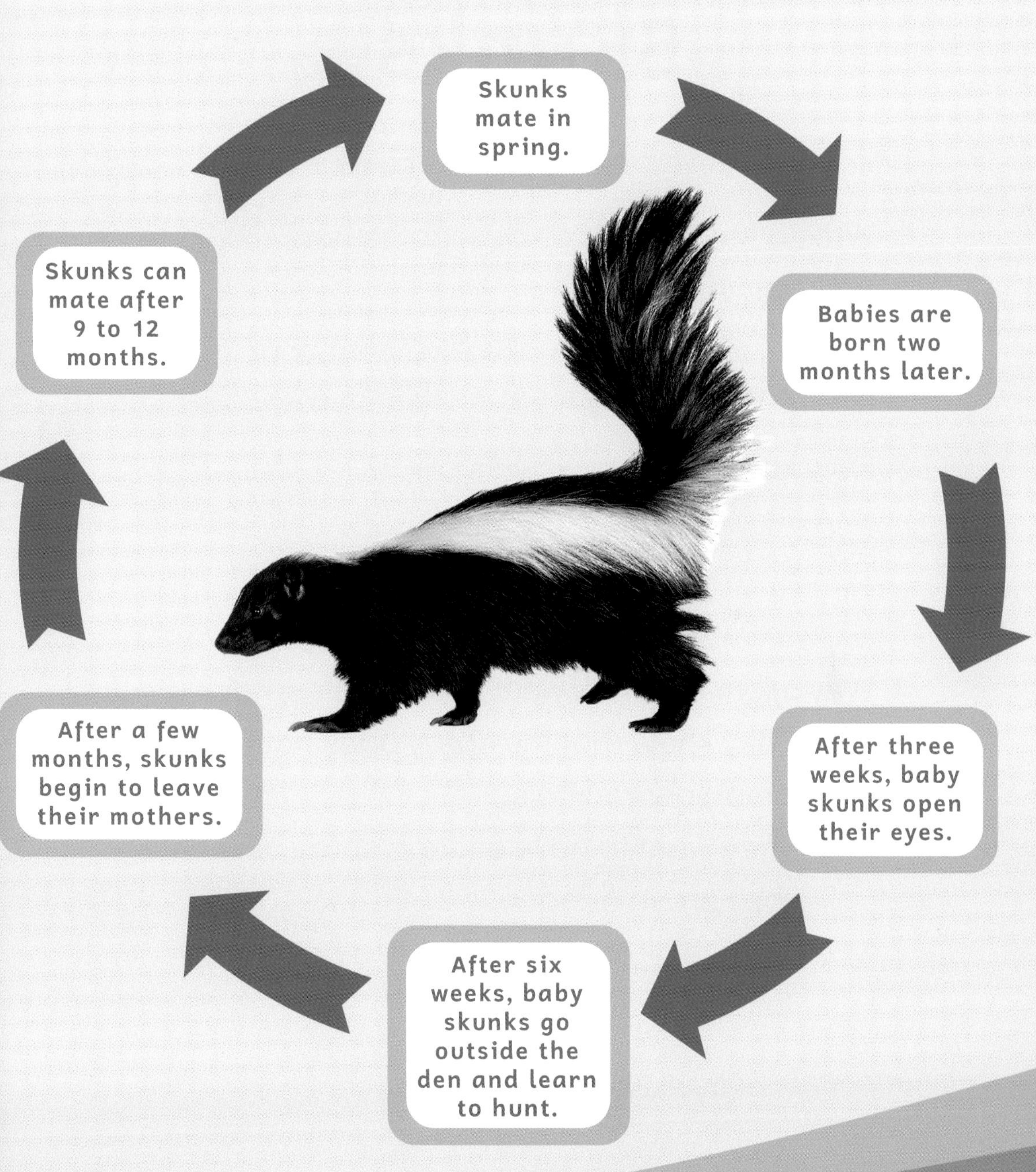
Skunks mate in spring.
Babies are born two months later.
After three weeks, baby skunks open their eyes.
After six weeks, baby skunks go outside the den and learn to hunt.
After a few months, skunks begin to leave their mothers.
Skunks can mate after 9 to 12 months.

FOCUS ON

Skunks

Write your answers on a separate piece of paper.

1. Write a few sentences describing how skunks use their spray.
2. Would you want a skunk to live near your home? Why or why not?
3. How long are baby skunks blind?
   - A. three weeks
   - B. six weeks
   - C. two months
4. Why might skunks try not to use their spray?
   - A. They know that the spray does not work on bigger animals.
   - B. They want to have enough spray next time they are in danger.
   - C. They think that stomping is a better way to blind predators.

Answer key on page 24.

Glossary

blind
To make an animal unable to see.

dens
Holes or tunnels that animals use as their homes.

glands
Organs in the body that make chemicals.

liquid
Not solid or gas.

litters
Groups of babies born to a mother at one time.

mammals
Animals that have hair and feed their babies milk.

mate
To come together to make a baby.

predator
An animal that hunts other animals for food.

To Learn More

BOOKS

Downs, Kieran, *Skunk vs. Raccoon*. Minneapolis: Bellwether Media, 2023.

Statts, Leo. *Skunks*. Minneapolis: Abdo Publishing, 2020.

NOTE TO EDUCATORS

Visit **www.focusreaders.com** to find lesson plans, activities, links, and other resources related to this title.

Index

Answer Key: 1. Answers will vary; **2.** Answers will vary; **3.** A; **4.** B